The Pannier Papers

4. The 57XX engines: 87XX, 96XX, 97XX

Ian Sixsmith

Richard Derry

Irwell Press Ltd.

Acknowledgements

Thanks to Eric Youldon, Allan C. Baker, Don Townsley, David Russell, Mike Winstock, Stephen Whittaker, Andy Forster, George Reeve and Brian Penney for advice and assistance in the compilation of these notes.

First published in the United Kingdom in 2012
by Irwell Press Limited, 59A, High Street, Clophill,
Bedfordshire MK45 4BE
Tel: 01525 861888
Fax: 01525 862044
www.irwellpress.com

87XX

Pannier in the afternoon. 8700 (the second one, it will be recalled) shunting the goods yard alongside Tyseley station on 30 August 1958. GWR roundel still survives. Photograph Michael Mensing.

The second 8700 which included the cab and number plates of the original which was rebuilt as 9700, the first of the condensing locos. It now has a top feed boiler and small whistle shield; remarkably the old GWR button emblem is coming back from the dead on the pannier side, as seen in the distance in the previous picture. Interesting for once to see the shutter and cab door in place. They kept out the draughts but the footplate of a 57XX was a warm place at the best of times and it had to be inclement indeed before they came into play. And that's how the whistle shield worked... Photograph www.transporttreasury.co.uk

8700 9/2/31; renumbered 9700 1/34 on rebuilding as a condensing loco
Second one! 8700 Tyseley 5/3/34; Oxley 3/4/37; Tyseley 1/5/37; w/d 2/62
8701 9/2/31; Kidderminster 14/3/31; Gloucester 6/4/35; Hereford 9/8/52; Kidderminster 21/2/59; Gloucester 18/4/59; w/d 3/63
8702 12/2/31; Swindon 14/3/31; St. Philips Marsh 12/1/35; St. Blazey 25/2/56; Newport Ebbw Jct 27/1/62; Hereford 6/4/63; w/d 5/64
8703 12/2/31;St. Philips Marsh 14/3/31; w/d 1/58
8704 16/2/31;Chester 14/3/31; Wellington 18/9/37; Chester 13/11/37; Croes Newydd 30/3/40; Stafford Road 7/1941; Stourbridge 8/1941; w/d 2/60
8705 16/2/31; Chester 14/3/31; Stourbridge 28/7/34; Oxley 11/11/39; Stafford Road 30/3/40; Aberbeeg 24/3/56; w/d 4/61
8706 20/2/31; Llanelly 14/3/31; Swansea Victoria 28/11/53; Llanelly 5/9/59; w/d 7/61
8707 20/2/31; Llanelly 14/3/31; Old Oak 4/3/39; Pontypool Road 3/12/55; w/d 7/64
8708 21/2/31; Llanelly 14/3/31; Landore 26/3/49; Llanelly 24/1/53; w/d 5/60
8709 21/2/31; Laira 14/3/31; St. Blazey 26/9/31; Exeter 21/11/31; Newton Abbot 15/12/34; St.Blazey 8/1/38; Laira 28/6/38; Taunton 7/1942; Laira 10/1942; Llanelly 10/7/48; Chester 13/12/58; Chester Midland 16/4/60; Pontypool Road 21/5/60; w/d 9/62
8710 26/2/31;Severn Tunnel Jct 11/4/31; Aberbeeg 24/8/35; Newport Ebbw Jct 9/1/37; Aberbeeg 11/1943; Newport Ebbw Jct 12/1945; Tondu 16/5/59; w/d 3/63
8711 26/2/31; Newport Ebbw Jct 11/4/31; Aberbeeg 24/10/31; Newport Ebbw Jct 8/4/32; Aberbeeg 7/5/32; Newport Ebbw Jct 30/7/32; Aberbeeg 27/8/32; Newport Ebbw Jct6/4/35; Aberbeeg 4/5/35; Newport Ebbw Jct 9/1/37; Tredegar 8/8/59; Newport Ebbw Jct 18/6/60; Swindon 8/10/60; w/d 3/62
8712 2/3/31; Pontypool Road 11/4/31; Aberbeeg 3/1943; Tondu 9/1944; w/d 1/63
8713 2/3/31; St. Philips Marsh 14/3/31; Yeovil 17/10/36; Westbury 14/11/36; St. Philips Marsh 13/11/37; Oxley 28/1/56; Tyseley 27/2/56; St.Blazey 3/10/56; Tyseley 28/11/59; w/d 3/62
8714 6/3/31; St. Philips Marsh 14/3/31; Westbury 22/8/36; Yeovil 8/1/38; Westbury 2/4/38; St. Philips Marsh 17/9/38; Bristol Bath Road 3/11/56; St. Philips Marsh 23/2/57; Westbury 12/8/61; st. Philips Marsh 2/12/61; Duffryn Yard 11/8/62; Swansea East Dock 9/2/63; w/d 11/64
8715 6/3/31; Llanelly 14/3/31; Danygraig 19/11/32; Llanelly 17/12/32; Neath 21/9/35; w/d 4/62
8716 12/3/31; Tondu 14/3/31; Severn tunnel Jct 7/5/32; Cardiff Canton 30/7/32; Severn Tunnel Jct 27/8/32; Tondu 22/9/34;Aberbeeg 9/1/1944; Pontypool Road 17/5/47; w/d 4/64
8717 12/3/31; Gloucester 14/3/31; Worcester by 12/1933; Gloucester 5/5/34; Kidderminster 2/5/36; Gloucester 25/7/36; Kidderminster then Gloucester 11/1946; Abercynon 27/1/62; w/d 7/64
8718 16/3/31; Gloucester 14/3/31; Worcester 9/3/35; Kidderminster 19/10/35; Worcester 1/4/39; Kidderminster 29/4/39; Gloucester 7/1946; Kidderminster 8/1946; Stourbridge 5/9/64; Shrewsbury 16/7/66; w/d 7/66
8719 16/3/31; Newton Abbot 14/3/31; St. Blazey 12/1932; Newton Abbot by 12/1933; Laira 12/1/35; Newton Abbot 11/11/39; Laira 4/1940; St. Blazey 5/1940; Laira 8/1941; Taunton 12/7/58; St. Blazey 21/1/59; w/d 5/62
8720 20/3/31; Danygraig 9/5/31; Swansea Victoria 26/1/52; Danygraig 23/2/52; Didcot 26/12/59; w/d 9/64
8721 20/3/31; Reading 9/5/31; Llantrisant by 12/1933; Aberbeeg 8/1942; Tondu 6/1943; w/d 7/61
8722 26/3/31; Westbury 9/5/31; St. Philips Marsh 25/8/34; Slough 7/10/50; Cardiff East Dock 19/6/54; Worcester 10/8/57; Hereford 9/8/58; Cardiff Canton 18/6/60; w/d 4/61
8723 26/3/31; Newport Ebbw Jct 9/5/31; Aberbeeg 6/6/31; Pill 21/9/35; Aberbeeg 12/11/38; Cardiff Canton 10/7/48; Merthyr 16/6/62; Aberbeeg 9/2/63; Merthyr 9/3/63; Aberdare 7/5/63; w/d 7/64
8724 30/3/31; Pontypool Road 9/5/31; Newport Ebbw Jct 3/4/37; Pontypool Road 3/4/37; Newport Ebbw Jct 12/1940; Aberbeeg 26/1/46; Aberdare 31/10/53; Danygraig 6/11/54; Duffryn Yard 28/11/59; w/d 7/62
8725 27/11/30; Birkenhead 30/12/30; Stourbridge by 12/1933; Tyseley 15/12/34; Leamington Spa 4/3/39; Tyseley 1/4/39; Leamington Spa 11/11/39; Tyseley 3/2/40; Stafford Road 7/1941; Birkenhead 8/1941; Tyseley 9/9/50; Wrexham Rhosddu 27/12/58; Bristol Barrow Road 21/1/59; w/d 10/62
8726 8/12/30; Tyseley 30/12/30; Stafford Road 17/9/38; Kidderminster 12/6/48; Stafford Road 10/7/48; Llanelly 16/7/60; w/d 4/61
8727 15/12/30; Reading 30/12/30; Old Oak 14/2/31; Hereford 10/2/34; Kidderminster 17/11/34; Worcester 10/12/38; Kidderminster 7/1/39; Gloucester 20/4/57; Croes Newydd 1/11/58; w/d 4/62
8728 22/12/30;Old Oak 17/1/31; Aberbeeg by 12/1933; Newport Ebbw Jct 9/1/37; Cardiff Canton 8/1942; Barry 8/9/62; Cardiff East Dock 9/2/63; Aberdare 20/4/63; Nine Elms 24/6/63; w/d 7/63
8729 2/1/31; Old Oak 17/1/31; Wellington 10/2/34; Stourbridge 16/11/35; Shrewsbury 23/7/38; Stafford Road 15/10/38; Shrewsbury 12/11/38; Oxley 12/1939; Banbury 3/2/40; Chester 11/8/51; Chester Midland 16/4/60; Gloucester 21/5/60; w/d 12/62
8730 2/2/31; St. Philips Marsh 14/3/31; Westbury 6/3/37; St. Philips Marsh 16/10/37; Chester 29/12/56; Chester Midland 16/4/60; Croes Newydd 21/5/60; Abercynon 18/6/60; w/d 7/62
8731 3/2/31; Kidderminster 14/3/31; Worcester 6/3/37; Kidderminster 3/4/37; Worcester 2/4/38; Gloucester 4/2/39; Worcester 30/12/50; Gloucester 24/3/51; Hereford 24/3/51; Kidderminster 16/5/53; Gloucester 8/10/55; Southall 3/12/60; w/d 7/62
8732 16/2/31; Neath 14/3/31; Danygraig 24/10/31; Llanelly 25/8/34; Landore 25/12/48; Llanelly 8/10/49; Neath 26/1/57; Swansea East Dock 31/12/63; w/d 4/64
8733 23/2/31; Gloucester 11/4/31; Old Oak 9/4/32; St. Philips Marsh 19/11/32; Swindon 27/6/36; St. Blazey 29/12/51; w/d 2/62
8734 2/3/31; Chester 11/4/31; Oxley 10/3/34; Chester 7/4/34; Stafford Road 6/1940; Oxley 7/1940; Stafford Road 10/1940; Oxley 11/1940; Stafford Road 4/1942; Wrexham Rhosddu 1/11/58; Croes Newydd 30/1/60; w/d 3/62
8735 17/3/31; Aberbeeg 9/5/31; Newport Ebbw Jct 1/8/31; Gloucester 8/1940; Barry 31/12/49; Abercynon 29/11/58; w/d 1/62
8736 24/3/31; Merthyr 4/7/31; Barry 27/7/35; Merthyr 24/8/35; Cathays 16/11/35; Rhymney 5/3/38; Cathays 2/4/38; Merthyr 15/10/38; Cathays 10/12/38; Abercynon 3/2/40; Merthyr 3/11/45; Llanelly 21/2/59; w/d 3/62
8737 7/4/31; Brecon 9/5/31; St. Philips Marsh 14/11/36; Westbury 5/3/38; St. Philips Marsh 16/5/59; Tyseley 13/6/59; St. Blazey 3/10/59; Neath 19/5/62; w/d 12/62
8738 14/4/31;Cardiff Canton 9/5/31; Llantrisant 27/6/36; Cardiff Canton 25/7/36; Pontypool Road 19/9/36; Cardiff Canton 14/11/36; Merthyr 21/8/37; Cardiff Canton 4/2/39; Aberbeeg 6/1942; Didcot 10/1943; Old Oak 20/4/46; Llanelly 4/9/48; Neyland 13/6/53; Swansea Victoria 28/11/53; Neyland 30/1/54; w/d 3/63
8739 23/4/31;Newport Ebbw Jct 6/6/31; Aberbeeg 3/1941; Newport Ebbw Jct 4/1941; Aberbeeg 10/1944; Cardiff Canton 1/12/45; Aberbeeg 13/7/46; Llantrisant 25/2/50; Neyland 8/10/55; Fishguard Goodwick 14/7/62; Swansea East Dock 31/12/63; Oxley 16/5/64; w/d 11/64
8740 12/5/31; Reading 4/7/31; Tondu 22/9/34; Barry 11/11/39; Tondu 12/1939; Aberbeeg 6/1943; Cardiff Canton 1/12/45; Tondu 17/6/50; w/d 2/61
8741 18/5/31; Swindon 6/6/31; St. Philips Marsh 28/7/34; Bristol Bath Road 13/7/57; St. Philips Marsh 10/9/60; w/d 5/62
8742 27/5/31; Reading 4/7/31; Gloucester 5/5/34; Worcester 20/8/38; Stafford Road 1/1940; Stourbridge 2/1940; w/d 9/62
8743 5/6/31;Cardiff Canton 4/7/31; Llantrisant 10/2/34; Cardiff East Dock 10/1942; Worcester 10/8/57; Swansea Victoria 7/9/57 Worcester 5/10/57; Hereford 1/11/58; Gloucester 21/2/59; Old Oak 27/1/64; w/d 6/64
8744 12/6/31; Westbury 6/6/31; St. Philips Marsh 6/1934; Westbury 13/11/37; Weymouth 21/2/53; Westbury 3/10/53; w/d 10/62

8745	22/6/31; Worcester 26/9/31; Old Oak 9/4/32; Westbury 19/11/32; St. Philips Marsh 6/4/35; Westbury 21/9/35; Yeovil 14/12/35; Westbury 22/8/36; Yeovil Pen Mill 7/8/48; Yeovil Town 12/1/59; Bath Green Park 30/11/63; Gloucester 5/10/64; w/d 8/65
8746	29/6/31; St. Philips Marsh 4/7/31; Westbury 4/5/35; Yeovil 22/8/36; Westbury 19/9/36; Yeovil 15/10/38; Westbury 12/11/38; St. Philips Marsh 3/1940; Weymouth 3/12/49; St. Philips Marsh 25/2/50; Duffryn Yard 3/11/62; w/d 12/62
8747	3/7/31; St. Philips Marsh 29/8/31; Westbury 4/5/35; Swindon 10/1939; Westbury 11/1939; St. Philips Marsh 10/1942; Bristol Bath Road 3/11/56; St. Philips Marsh 23/2/57; Bath Green Park 7/10/61; St. Philips Marsh 30/12/61; Neath 16/6/62; w/d 5/64
8748	9/7/31; Newport Ebbw Jct 29/8/31; Aberbeeg 14/12/35; Newport Ebbw Jct 9/1/37; Tondu 28/5/38; Newport Ebbw Jct 20/8/38; Tondu 17/9/38; Cardiff Canton 6/1941; Tondu 1/1942; Cardiff Canton 4/1942; Aberbeeg 11/1944; Tondu 12/1945; w/d 9/62
8749	13/7/31; Whitland 29/8/31; Landore 22/10/32; Llanelly 27/7/35; Gloucester 20/7/64; w/d 10/64
8750	Old Oak 9/31; Southall 27/12/52; Swansea East Dock 21/5/60; w/d 5/62
8751	Old Oak 10/33; Newport Ebbw Jct 23/4/60; w/d 12/62
8752	Old Oak 10/33; Southall 2/5/38; w/d 1/63
8753	Old Oak 10/33; Southall 6/2/37; Old Oak 3/4/37; w/d 2/62
8754	Old Oak 10/33; w/d 11/60
8755	Old Oak 10/33; Southall 21/8/37; Pontypool Road 11/1943; Old Oak 3/12/55; w/d 12/57
8756	Old Oak 10/33; w/d 10/62
8757	Southall 10/33; Old Oak 15/10/38; Didcot 11/1944; Old Oak 2/1946; w/d 9/62
8758	Oxford 11/33; Southall 24/7/37; w/d 1/59
8759	Old Oak 10/33; w/d 1/63
8760	Old Oak 10/33; Neath 23/4/60; w/d 1/62
8761	Old Oak 10/33; Southall 16/5/59; Oxford 27/2/60; Old Oak 10/9/60; w/d 5/62
8762	Old Oak 10/33; w/d 8/61
8763	Old Oak 10/33; w/d 8/62
8764	Old Oak 10/33; Southall 27/5/39; Old Oak 22/4/50; Barry 26/3/60; w/d 5/62
8765	Old Oak 13/1/34; w/d 9/62
8766	Reading 12/1933; Old Oak 10/2/34; St. Philips Marsh 1/4/39; Newport Ebbw Jct 30/1/54; w/d 7/63
8767	Old Oak 12/33; Oxley 27/7/63; Stourbridge 23/4/66; Croes Newydd 16/7/66; w/d 7/66
8768	Didcot 12/1933; Old Oak 10/2/34; w/d 9/64
8769	Old Oak 12/33; Southall 16/5/59; w/d 4/61
8770	Old Oak 13/1/34; Slough 13/8/60; Southall 25/3/61; w/d 12/62
8771	Old Oak 13/1/34; Reading 2/5/36; Old Oak 30/5/36; w/d 7/62
8772	Old Oak 13/1/34; Southall 10/2/34; Old Oak 4/5/35; Duffryn Yard 10/9/60; w/d 8/61
8773	Old Oak 13/1/34; w/d 10/62
8774	Southall 13/1/34; Swansea East Dock 21/5/60; Cardiff Canton 17/6/61; w/d 8/61
8775	Neath 13/1/34; w/d 12/61
8776	Pontypool Road 13/1/34; Aberbeeg 11/1/36; Pontypool Road 4/4/36; Aberbeeg 9/1944; Pontypool Road 10/1944; Aberbeeg 17/5/47; Cardiff Canton 22/3/52; Barry 8/9/62; w/d 12/62
8777	Newport Ebbw Jct 13/1/34; Pill 10/1941; Newport Ebbw Jct 11/1941; Aberbeeg 26/1/46; Tondu 9/8/47; Pontypool Road 3/10/53; Carmarthen 24/3/56; w/d 4/61
8778	Tondu 10/2/34; Aberbeeg 10/1942; Newport Ebbw Jct 26/1/46; w/d 8/60
8779	Westbury 10/2/34; St. Philips Marsh 6/3/37; Swindon 2/4/38; w/d 2/62
8780	Landore 10/2/34; Danygraig 18/9/37; Neath 3/2/40; Old Oak 17/5/47; Radyr 23/4/49; Barry 21/2/59; Radyr 16/5/59; w/d 7/62
8781	Llanelly 10/2/34; Brecon 22/8/36; Hereford 24/7/37; Gloucester 29/4/39; Hereford 23/2/57; Pontypool Road 19/5/62; Newport Ebbw Jct 8/9/62; w/d 12/62
8782	Neath 10/2/34; Llanelly 9/9/61; w/d 11/61
8783	St.Blazey 10/2/34; Penzance 30/3/40; Swindon 29/12/51; Taunton 19/5/62; Llanelly 9/2/63; w/d 6/63
8784	Tyseley 10/2/34; Neath 30/12/50; w/d 4/62
8785	Landore 10/2/34; Llanelly 8/9/45; w/d 12/63
8786	Newport Ebbw Jct 1/34; Aberbeeg 30/5/36; Newport Ebbw Jct 9/1/37; Cardiff Canton 4/1941; Aberbeeg 2/1943; Newport Ebbw Jct 7/1944; Aberdare 25/2/50; Pontypool Road 7/10/50; Aberbeeg 27/12/52; Neyland 30/11/57; Aberbeeg 19/4/58; Nine Elms 24/6/63; w/d 7/63
8787	Stourbridge 10/2/34; Stafford Road 28/5/38; Stourbridge 4/3/39; Banbury 10/1942; Cardiff East Dock 16/7/55; Worcester 10/8/57; Swansea Victoria 7/9/57; Worcester 5/10/57; Hereford 9/8/58; w/d 8/61
8788	Aberbeeg 10/2/34; Newport Ebbw Jct 9/1/37; Pontypool Road 20/8/38; Landore 21/4/56; Neath 18/6/60; w/d 5/62
8789	Landore 10/3/34; w/d 6/61
8790	St. Philips Marsh 10/3/34; Westbury 16/10/37; St. Philips Marsh 5/1942; Swindon 8/1944; St. Philips Marsh 10/1944; w/d 5/62
8791	Stourbridge 7/4/34; Stafford Road 4/5/35; Stourbridge 1/6/35; Stafford Road 11/12/37; Stourbridge by 12/1940; Croes Newydd 11/8/56; Hereford 25/3/61; Pill 17/6/61; Neath 19/5/62; w/d 3/63
8792	Stafford Road 10/3/34; Oxley 6/1934; Stourbridge 5/2/38; w/d 2/62
8793	St. Philips Marsh 7/4/34; Swindon 10/7/48; Weymouth 17/7/54; Swindon 9/10/54; Worcester 9/3/63; w/d 12/64
8794	Newport Ebbw Jct 7/4/34; Cardiff Canton 11/1944; Aberbeeg 20/4/46; Newport Ebbw Jct 24/1/53; Landore 11/8/56; Swansea East Dock 17/6/61; Nine Elms 24/6/63; w/d 7/63
8795	Bristol Bath Road 7/4/34; Westbury 7/1/39; St. Philips Marsh 4/2/39; Swindon 8/1944; St. Philips Marsh 11/1944; Bristol Bath Road 16/6/56; St. Philips Marsh 4/10/58; Bristol Barrow Road 3/11/62; w/d 7/65
8796	Llantrisant 7/4/34; Newport Ebbw Jct 28/5/38; Aberbeeg 1/43; Newport Ebbw Jct 2/1945; Pill 31/12/49; Aberbeeg 20/4/57; Stafford Road 4/10/58; w/d 4/61
8797	Tyseley 5/5/34; Banbury 3/1943; Stourbridge 4/1943; w/d 4/62
8798	Oxley 5/5/34; Stafford Road 15/10/38; Oxley 12/11/38; Stafford Road 16/5/53; Swansea East Dock 21/5/60; w/d 6/61
8799	Pontypool Road 25/8/34; Severn Tunnel Jct 28/5/38; Weymouth 11/8/56; w/d 11/62

First fifty 8700-8749, first dates are 'Arrived at factory'

5

18 March 1962 at Swindon and unbelievably the GWR roundel went to the grave with its loco; 8700 and 4632 are by now withdrawn and were scrapped in May 1962 at Swindon. Photograph Terry Nicholls.

A bright and shiny 8704 at Cardiff Cathays shed; it looks as if it could be fresh from overhaul, there is no shed plate and it was at Stourbridge all its BR life, so perhaps it has been to Barry works and is on its way back. Photograph Paul Chancellor Collection.

A pair of panniers at Swindon shed fresh out of the works; a 94XX directly behind 8707. Note how the route availability/ power class disc can be nearer to the numberplate on some engines than others... Coal typically on the cab roof; this will be tidied away by the fireman before leaving shed. Beyer Peacock plate on splasher; simple vertical welds on panniers. Notice the long cord hanging down from the gas lamp to turn it on/off when required. Photograph J.T. Clewley, www.transporttreasury.co.uk.

That glory of the facade that stared out across the main line at Swindon; just look at the broad gauge mouldings in the wall on 24 March 1963. 8710 had just been withdrawn from Tondu shed and was scrapped in May at Swindon. It's interesting for the tank which has had a new bottom welded in, as a result of corrosion – bottoms of tanks, where all the muck accumulated, tended to require renewal sooner. There are three, rather cruder, upright welds too. You can't really rely on any tank being the same as another... Photograph Stephen Gradidge.

Panniers at St Blazey, a more or less unique semi-roundhouse, originally built by the Cornwall Minerals Railway. 8713 is stabled on one of the roads on 5 June 1959 during the short period it was based there. Alongside are a couple of 16XXs – see *Pannier Papers No.5*. Photograph Paul Chancellor Collection.

8718 at Kidderminster shed on 2 September 1962. The cab windows swivelled for cleaning purposes and it was fairly usual to see them half open like this. This was one of the last 57XXs to be withdrawn, in July 1966, having moved to Shrewsbury the same month. It was the last in service with the old style cab. Photograph Stephen Gradidge.

8720 at Danygraig shed; 'BR grey' livery, no trace of emblem. Original pattern of injector this side with distinct absence of visible piping; it would have been the same story the other side. Photograph J. Davenport, Initial Photographics.

8723 at Cardiff General on 30 August 1956 on duty H15. Wonderful art deco-ish tower and advert for Pirelli Tyres in the background; note also the 'Cordon' gas tanks used to 'charge' gas to dining cars and sleeping cars. This was one of more than 150 of the class reportedly disposed of by Cashmores, Newport. Photograph Stephen Gradidge.

8723 at Cardiff Canton; earlier style injector again; the 'R' of GWR clinging to life. Photograph J. Davenport, Initial Photographics.

Cardiff General, like other major WR stations, saw a constant to and fro of trundling pannier tanks, 'coffee pots' to us unappreciative oiks. This is 8728 on the 'STATION 2' target on 28 August 1956 with, apparently, a missing whistle shield. It was one of the class that went late to Nine Elms shed, in June 1963 only to be withdrawn the following month. So it is presumed to be one of those infamous 'paper transfers'. Photograph Stephen Gradidge.

8738 in a corner of Swindon Works; vertical riveting, longitudinal weld on the pannier. Observe how the 'pep' pipe, hanging in the same place for years, has left a salt deposit/ruined paint down the cab side. Who would think to model that? It might well be withdrawn with that drift of steam/smoke coming from something on the far side; the smokebox dart handles are gone anyway. The 57XXs attracted a fair amount of chalked graffiti but this (observe the safety valve casing) is the first swastika to appear! When based at Didcot it had carried a spark arrester chimney. Photograph J.G. Walmsley, www.transporttreasury.co.uk

8745 with very prominently riveted panniers, at Yeovil Town shed on 27 July 1963. The engine resided there for nearly five years before moving on to Bath Green Park in November 1963, not long after Yeovil was taken over by the WR. Photograph Stephen Gradidge.

8751 on an empty stock job at Paddington, leaving for Old Oak on 4 March 1955; there was certainly no question (at least generally) of 'dolling' up the pilot engines that frequented Paddington. This one's a perfect disgrace, with GWR (well, part of the W and most of the R) still there, just. 8751 eventually moved to Ebbw Junction, in April 1960. Photograph Stephen Gradidge.

8752 at Southall shed on 27 October 1962; this was its home for a number of years until withdrawal in January 1963. Whitened smokebox door straps, after the habit of the time. On visits to Southall in steam days, 8752 always seemed to be on shed. Photograph Stephen Gradidge.

One of Old Oak's long-term residents, 8756, at home on 5 March 1960. Photograph Peter Groom.

Swindon on 12 August 1962 with 8764, withdrawn but in 'on arrival' condition. As can be seen, it was quite possible (likely, even) for a 57XX to reach withdrawal still bearing the first emblem. Photograph Stephen Gradidge.

8765, another of Old Oak's 'regulars' near the coaling stage on 17 August 1962, keeping the first emblem (or a remnant of it at least) to the end. Photograph Peter Groom.

Canton's 8766 works into Cardiff General on 29 August 1956, with what looks like empty stock – the headlamps indicate a carriage pilot. Photograph Stephen Gradidge.

A selection of the higher numbered 87XX series were based at Old Oak in the last days of WR steam; 8767, with typically stowed shovel, was one of them on 19 May 1963. It moved away to Oxley a few weeks later and eventually ended its time as one of 'the last' at Croes Newydd shed in July 1966. Photograph Stephen Gradidge.

8768 coming into Paddington with empty stock on Saturday 1 September 1962. Target No.3, correct ECS headlamp code; it is on the last few yards of No.2 Up Engine & Carriage line, bound for a higher-numbered departure platform – up to No.6. This picture first appeared in *British Railways Illustrated* December 2009 – *Empty Stock Working at Paddington*. Author Christopher Tanous, who worked (unofficially) many of these trains, notes: 'As was common, the driver, still quite a young man, has put on a bit of weight since his fairly recent days of being a very fit and lean top-link fireman! There is a wisp of steam from the injector exhaust under the cab steps, perhaps revealing that the fireman is anxious to reduce pressure by using the second injector to get plenty of cold water into the boiler, just at blowing off point, before they go under the overall roof for half an hour on the buffer stops'. Photograph Stephen Gradidge.

8768 a year so later, at Old Oak shed on 21 July 1963. Withdrawal came in September 1964 and disposal in South Wales the following April. Photograph Stephen Gradidge.

Lining at last! 8771, which carried the black livery lined out in red, cream and gray, at Old Oak Common on 4 March 1956. It didn't really suit them but in this dirty condition it hardly matters. The intended effect was that Paddington pilots should look a bit better than the average filthy 'tankie' but it needed more effort than this to keep up the show. Photograph Peter Groom.

Southall's 8774 passing West Ealing on 12 March 1955 with a local train. It later moved to South Wales and was broken up at Swindon at the end of 1961. Photograph Stephen Gradidge.

Around the turntable once again at Swindon, 24 March 1963. The practice of sending locos up to main works for a decision as to repair/condemning meant engines like 8776, though withdrawn, are still the same running condition in which they made the last journey. Someone's pinched that whistle shield, though... Photograph Stephen Gradidge.

8776 at Canton; top feed boiler and larger whistle shield, steam heating.

8778 at what looks like Aberbeeg and a bout of shunting in the rain. Photograph Paul Chancellor Collection.

Another condemnee. 8791 at Swindon on 26 May 1963, fate awaited. Someone is taking the mickey with the chalked XL5 (as in *Fireball XL5*, which managed to be both a childrens TV puppet show and a lolly). Barely-visible second BR emblem, further forward than usual. Photograph Stephen Gradidge.

8799 newly outshopped at Caerphilly Works on 20 September 1959, in that striking mirror-finish black. The works in fact had a penchant for painting the cabside number figures and the surround in cream. The NOT TO BE MOVED sign might mean it has yet to complete a steam test – note the strange lance and piping leaning on the far side of the loco appearing to rest on the top of the chimney. It's a long way from its home shed Weymouth and Caerphilly would be a most unexpected place to find a Southern loco...

96XX

9606 shunting at Gloucester Central on 10 October 1964. This would certainly be a weathering challenge for any modeller! It seems that only in Britain was steam treated with some odd form of deliberate contempt in the final years, with the railway delighting, almost, in open neglect. Mind you, most of the diesels were hardly better cared for. An out of gauge shovel? Photograph B.K.B. Green Collection, Initial Photographics.

9615 outside the little shed at Frome, an outstation of Westbury, in the 1950s. A tiny one road, single locomotive shed with virtually no siding accommodation, it nevertheless had up to a dozen pannier tanks working freight and passenger trains in the district. The faithful are paying their respects. Photograph Paul Chancellor Collection.

9600 Swindon 3/45; St. Philips Marsh 22/4/61; Aberdare 3/11/62; Neath 7/11/64; Newport Ebbw Jct. 15/5/65; w/d 9/65; Engine preserved
9601 Yeovil 5/45; Weymouth 24/3/56; St. Philips Marsh 20/4/57; Bristol Barrow Road 31/12/63; w/d 12/64
9602 Fishguard Goodwick 6/45; Treherbert 31/8/63; Pontypool Road 6/3/65; w/d 3/65
9603 Fishguard Goodwick 6/45; Cardiff Canton 6/11/54; Barry 8/9/62; Cardiff East Dock 9/2/63; Barry 2/11/63; w/d 12/63
9604 St. Philips Marsh 6/45; Bristol Bath Road 22/3/52; Swindon 26/2/55; w/d 12/62
9605 St. Philips Marsh 6/45; Swindon 21/4/56; Westbury 28/11/64; w/d 9/65
9606 St. Philips Marsh 7/45; Danygraig 27/3/54; Carmarthen 7/9/57; Swansea East Dock 27/7/63; Gloucester Horton Road 20/7/64; Bristol Barrow Road 5/10/64; Gloucester Horton Road 26/10/64; w/d 11/64
9607 Shrewsbury 7/45; Aberdare 26/1/46; w/d 4/64
9608 Tyseley 7/45; Stafford Road 30/10/48; Tyseley 27/11/48; Taunton 2/11/57; Croes Newydd 3/11/62; Stourbridge 28/11/64; w/d 7/66
9609 Aberdare 7/45; Tondu 23/2/57; Neath 4/5/64; Llanelly 15/5/65; w/d 10/65
9610 Tyseley 8/45; Bristol Bath Road 31/10/3; St. Philips Marsh 23/2/57; Wrexham Rhosddu 1/11/58; Croes Newydd 30/1/60; w/d 9/66
9611 Oxford 8/9/45; Pontypool Road 10/9/60; Treherbert 8/9/62; Radyr 7/11/64; w/d 4/65
9612 Westbury 8/9/45; w/d 12/63
9613 Stourbridge 6/10/45; Tyseley 17/4/48; Stourbridge 15/5/48; w/d 10/65
9614 Brecon 6/10/45; Croes Newydd 23/4/49; Tyseley 25/6/49; Leamington Spa 26/12/59; Tyseley 30/1/60; Stourbridge 9/9/61; w/d 7/66
9615 Westbury 6/10/45; Yeovil 27/12/47; Westbury 23/4/49; St. Philips Marsh 30/12/61; Duffryn Yard 3/11/62; Neath 13/4/64; Aberdare 6/2/65; Radyr 27/3/65; w/d 7/65
9616 Llantrisant 1/12/45; Newport Ebbw Jct 23/3/46; Severn Tunnel Jct 5/10/64; w/d 8/65
9617 Duffryn Yard 3/11/45; Neath 13/4/64; w/d 6/65
9618 Merthyr 3/11/45; w/d 12/63
9619 Hereford 3/11/45; Severn Tunnel Jct 6/9/58; w/d 7/65
9620 St. Philips Marsh 3/11/45; Weymouth 4/11/50; Bristol Barrow Road 29/9/63; Gloucester Horton Road 2/11/63; w/d 7/64
9621 Stafford Road 1/12/45; Croes Newydd 27/12/58; Wellington 26/12/59; Llanelly 28/161; w/d 10/64
9622 Merthyr 1/12/45; Barry 16/7/55; Abercynon 29/11/58; Radyr 7/11/64; w/d 7/65
9623 Taunton 29/12/45; Newton Abbot 15/6/46; Bristol Bath Road 21/5/55; St. Philips Marsh 10/9/60; Bristol Barrow Road 3/11/62; w/e 7/65
9624 Wellington 1/12/45; Stourbridge 3/12/55; w/d 1/65
9625 Swansea East Dock 1/12/45; Landore 26/1/46; Swansea East Dock 23/3/46; Neath 19/5/62; w/d 6/65
9626 St. Philips Marsh 29/12/45; Weymouth 23/3/57; St. Philips Marsh 18/5/57; Bristol Bath Road 2/11/57; St. Philips Marsh 10/9/60; Bristol Barrow Road 3/11/62; Worcester 18/9/65; w/d 12/65
9627 Neath 29/112/45; w/d 7/62
9628 Weymouth 29/12/45; Westbury 19/4/47; w/d 3/63
9629 Cardiff Canton 7/9/46; Exeter 11/7/53; Oswestry 21/5/60; Cardiff East Dock 15/12/62; Pontypool Road 4/5/64; w/d 10/64; Engine preserved
9630 Wellington 26/1/46; Worcester 8/10/60; Wellington 5/11/60; Croes Newydd 5/9/64; w/d 9/66
9631 Barry 26/1/46; Abercynon 22/2/47; Barry 23/3/47; Cathays 23/4/49; Barry 21/5/49; Merthyr 1/11/58; Neath 7/11/64; Llanelly 15/5/65; w/d 6/65
9632 Newport Ebbw Jct 26/1/46; Carmarthen 21/4/56; Llanelly 13/4/64; Abercynon 20/7/64; w/d 11/64
9633 Newton Abbot 23/2/46; Exeter 27/1/62; Duffryn Yard 8/9/62; w/d 10/63
9634 Duffryn Yard 26/1/46; Neath 13/4/64; w/d 5/64
9635 Tyseley 23/2/46; Exeter 24/3/62; Taunton 6/4/63; w/d 6/64
9636 Stourbridge 23/2/46; Wellington 10/9/60; w/d 10/63
9637 Newport Ebbw Jct 23/2/46; Landore 24/3/56; Llanelly 17/6/61; Neath 24/2/64; w/d 9/64
9638 Merthyr 23/2/46; Abercynon 29/11/47; Merthyr 7/8/48; w/d 12/63
9639 Wellington 23/2/46; Croes Newydd 5/9/64; w/d/9/65
9640 Slough 23/3/46; Oxford 7/10/50; Old Oak 3/12/60; Stafford Road 27/7/63; Oxley 10/8/63; w/d/7/66
9641 Southall 23/3/46; Shrewsbury 27/7/63; Stourbridge 28/11/64; Croes Newydd 16/7/66; w/d 1066
9642 Westbury 20/4/46; Swindon 18/5/46; Weymouth 22/3/47; Westbury 7/8/48; Weymouth 4/9/48; Abercynon 29/12/56; St. Philips Marsh 14/6/58; Southall 18/4/59; Old Oak 24/8/64; w/d 11/64; Engine preserved
9643 Merthyr 17/5/46; w/d 5/62
9644 Newport Ebbw Jct 17/5/46; Pontypool Road 30/11/63; Radyr 15/5/65; w/d 6/65
9645 Swansea East Dock 17/5/46; Swansea Victoria 30/11/57; Danygraig 25/1/58; Carmarthen 11/7/59; Fishguard Goodwick 30/1/60; w/d 10/63
9646 Newton Abbot 17/5/46; Exeter 13/7/46; Taunton 23/4/50; Stourbridge 21/4/62; w/d 5/65
9647 Exeter 13/7/46; Taunton 21/4/51; Exmouth Jct 5/10/64; Templecombe 12/6/65; w/d 6/65
9648 Cardiff Canton 13/7/46; Barry 8/9/62; Cardiff East Dock 9/2/63; Tondu 6/4/63; Neath 4/5/64; Llanelly 22/6/64; w/d 7/64
9649 Tondu 10/8/46; Merthyr 2/11/63; Newport Ebbw Jct 7/11/64; w/d 7/65
9650 Pontypool Road 13/7/46; w/d 12/64
9651 Birkenhead 10/8/46; Wrexham Rhosddu 27/12/58; Templecombe 21/1/59; St. Philips Marsh 18/4/59; Cardiff East Dock 6/10/62; w/d 7/65
9652 Neyland 30/11/46; Llanelly 27/12/58; w/d 1/63
9653 Slough 30/11/46; Oxford 13/6/53; w/d 7/65
9654 Oxford 30/11/46; w/d 10/64
9655 St. Blazey 28/12/46; Pontypool Road 19/5/62; w/d 5/64
9656 Croes Newydd 28/12/46; Shrewsbury 17/4/48; Duffryn Yard 15/12/62; Neath 13/4/64; Radyr 15/5/65; Severn Tunnel Jct 7/8/65; w/d 11/65
9657 Shrewsbury 30/11/46; Croes Newydd 20/3/48; Shrewsbury 15/5/48; w/d 4/66
9658 Old Oak 30/11/46; Stafford Road 27/7/63; Oxley 10/8/63; w/d 10/66
9659 Old Oak 28/12/46; w/d 6/65
9660 Tondu 28/12/46; Bristol Barrow Road 27/7/63; Swansea East Dock 27/1/64; Neath 22/6/64; w/d 11/64
9661 Old Oak 28/12/46; Stafford Road 27/7/63; Oxley 10/8/63; w/d 11/64
9662 Newport Ebbw Jct 15/5/48; Tredegar 11/7/59; Newport Ebbw Jct 21/5/60; w/d 9/65
9663 Taunton 17/4/48; w/d 9/64
9664 Newport Ebbw Jct 10/7/48; Newport Pill 12/1/63; w/d 5/64
9665 St. Philips Marsh 15/5/48; Penzance 27/2/54; Hereford 4/12/54; w/d 2/63
9666 Neath 15/5/48; Carmarthen 1/11/52; Fishguard Goodwick 5/10/57; Treherbert 31/8/63; Newport Ebbw Jct 6/3/65; w/d 9/65
9667 Newport Ebbw Jct 15/5/48; Abercynon 4/5/64; Radyr 7/11/64; w/d 6/65
9668 Newton Abbot 12/6/48; Exeter 16/7/55; Newton Abbot 10/9/55; Westbury 9/8/58; St. Philips Marsh 24/2/62; Abercynon 3/11/62; w/d 12/63
9669 Croes Newydd 12/6/48; Duffryn Yard 19/5/62; Croes Newydd 24/8/64; w/d 1/66
9670 Taunton 12/6/48; Templecombe 5/10/64; Yeovil Town 15/5/65; w/d 6/65
9671 Laira 12/6/48; Taunton 23/4/55 Duffryn Yard 31/12/60; Aberdare 9/3/63; Cardiff East Dock 22/6/64; w/d 3/65
9672 Shrewsbury 10/7/48; Swindon 16/6/56; Abercynon 24/8/64; w/d 12/65
9673 Laira 26/2/49; St. Blazey 24/3/51; w/d 5/60
9674 Tondu 26/2/49; Newport Ebbw Jct 5/9/53; Westbury 3/11/62; w/d 4/64
9675 Merthyr 26/3/49; Swansea East Dock 4/5/64; Neath 22/6/64; Radyr 15/5/65; Newport Ebbw Jct 7/8/65; w/d 10/65
9676 Cathays 26/3/49; Barry 21/5/49; Merthyr 29/11/58; Cardiff East Dock 26/10/64; w/d 6/65
9677 Cardiff East Dock 26/3/49; Fishguard Goodwick 7/9/57; Swansea East Dock 31/12/63; Neath 22/6/64; Llanelly 20/7/64; w/d 11/64
9678 Newton Abbot 23/4/49; Tondu 6/10/62; Newport Ebbw Jct 30/11/63; Aberdare 13/4/64; Swansea East Dock 4/65/64; Neath 22/6/64; Cardiff East Dock 12/6/65; w/d 6/65
9679 Cardiff East Dock 23/4/49; Cathays 30/11/57; Merthyr 1/11/58; w/d 11/64
9680 Tyseley 21/5/49; St. Blazey 16/7/60; Swindon 24/2/62; Worcester 7/11/64; Bristol Barrow Road 6/3/65; Gloucester Horton Road 6/11/65; w/d 12/65
9681 Tondu 21/5/49; Oswestry 21/4/56; Cardiff Canton 31/12/60; Barry 8/9/62; Cardiff East Dock 9/2/63; w/d 8/65; Engine preserved
9682 Tyseley 21/5/49; Aberbeeg 16/7/60; Radyr 7/11/64; w/d 8/65; Engine preserved

A typically grimy pannier, 9618 at its 88D Merthyr home.

And a perfectly respectable 57XX, 9618 at Merthyr in April 1958. Something about that rodding and piping allied to that (admittedly this is pushing it a bit) modernistic cab rather overcame the impression conveyed by that determinedly Victorian 'top layer' – voluptuous dome, extravagant safety valve bonnet and tapering chimney. Photograph J. Davenport, Initial Photographics.

A much more pleasing Swindon scene. 9631, completed in December 1945, is back at its birthplace on 26 May 1963 after a major overhaul. During visits to these works few of us dreamed that so many locos in this condition would have their working lives ended so soon. This one finished its days at Llanelly shed. Photograph Stephen Gradidge.

A fine-looking 9634 at Duffryn Yard shed; padlocked box, second emblem. Photograph J. Davenport, Initial Photographics.

9635 after repair at Swindon, on 24 March 1963; from here it went to Taunton. Welded repair patch on pannier. This was its first repaint since building in January 1946, only for it to be withdrawn a year or so later! Photograph Stephen Gradidge.

9639 waiting to leave Wellington with the 5.50pm to Much Wenlock, 21 April 1962. Good view of shutter and bunker doors, closed against the wet. There was 25kV not too far away, hence the electrification flashes. Photograph Michael Mensing.

9642 at Southall shed on 16 October 1960. It was sold in November 1964 to the NCB and eventually found its way into preservation. Photograph J. Davenport, Initial Photographics.

Stourbridge Junction where the shed painter obviously had time on his hands; 9646 was in woeful condition but though all the plates have been pinched/removed the unknown hero has tried to give the engine some dignity by painting on its running numbers, making a fair stab at replicating the GW style. The 2C shed code is correct as this former GWR shed was now under LMR control. The loco at the rear would be 2-6-2T 4151 which moved to 2C in March 1965 and was condemned the following month with 9646 following in the May. Photograph J. Davenport, Initial Photographics.

By contrast 9646 in an earlier life, shunting the ash road at Taunton and a joy to behold. Photograph J. Davenport, Initial Photographics.

Cardiff General and 9648 with target H16, busying itself around the station area with a good head of steam. Photograph Stephen Gradidge.

Splendid in black. A perfect 9648 at Swindon Works on 24 March 1963 on one of those turntable roads looking very pristine, especially compared with some of the malodorous examples we've seen so far. Photograph Stephen Gradidge.

Still glistening in the sunshine, 9648 was so attractive that Stephen Gradidge photographed the other side of it too. It awaits a shedplate but moved to Tondu shed and there then followed two more transfers before premature withdrawal in July 1964. Photograph Stephen Gradidge.

Late in the day for steam, 9653 is at Oxford shed on 15 May 1965, two months before withdrawal. The faintest of second emblems struggles through a formidable layer of grime. Photograph Stephen Gradidge.

9654 (date unknown but it bears the second emblem) at Lechlade with a train for Fairford; it was at Oxford shed all its life, so presumably was a fairly regular sight on the long branch. www.colourrail.co.uk

9654 on the Fairford branch at Witney, in June 1962. The train is obviously paused for a while, with the crew taking a break on the station bench. The water column was curiously sited halfway along the down platform and necessarily had a greatly elongated 'arm' but 9654 is heading towards Oxford. Operations at Witney were clearly not as straightforward as they might look... Photograph Paul Chancellor Collection.

Another pannier on a sleepy branch working. St Blazey's 9655 at Lostwithiel station and no doubt the crew are enjoying a quiet fag just out of view. This is the Fowey branch train in its usual position with one autocoach as normal. What isn't normal is to have a non-auto loco, requiring to run round after each trip. The regular 14XX obviously wasn't available. Photograph J. Davenport, Initial Photographics.

In amongst the ash and clinker of the Old Oak fire pits on 28 September 1963. 9658 had been at the great shed for years but by this time had moved to Stafford Road and Oxley in quick succession so something had brought it briefly back 'home'. It was finally withdrawn, from Oxley, in November 1966. Emblem well forward (that is, aligned with dome rather than middle wheels), older type boiler without tall top feed and a padlock on the toolbox. Photograph Stephen Gradidge.

9659 at the entrance to the Old Oak shed/carriage roads; the famous canal lurks behind that wall. Photograph J. Davenport, Initial Photographics.

9661 at Old Oak Common on 16 February 1958 which gives a good view of the vacuum piping that ran the length of the loco directly under the running plate. Connections and elbows made almost any configuration possible. 9661 was moved to Stafford Road in July 1963 and Oxley the next month and withdrawn November 1964. Photograph Peter Groom.

A bright 57XX in excellent condition, not long out of works no doubt; 9668 at Newton Abbot shed in the 1950s. Photograph Ted's Dad.

9669 with the seemingly obligatory three coaches, at Bala on 27 June 1962. A reminder that the tank end footsteps are fixed only at each end – daylight passes through the treadplate. On some it's possible to convince yourself that this is not the case – the steps are 'solid'. Moreover on earlier engines, as we've seen, the steps are simpler, flat things without the turned up ends, after the fashion of the lower steps on the smokebox front. Photograph Eric Sawford, www.transporttreasury.co.uk

Beautiful in black. 9672 obviously fresh from overhaul, at its home, Swindon shed, in July 1957.

9674, clean, bustling and with the usual three coaches, arrives at Princes End & Coseley station (near Tipton in Staffordshire) with the 11.7am Stourbridge Junction-Wolverhampton Low Level on Sunday 30 July 1961. Photograph Michael Mensing.

9677 on 13 March 1953 at Cardiff East Dock shed, closed in March 1958 and reopened in September 1962 while Canton was converted to diesels and finally closed in August 1965. 9677 spent a fair time at Goodwick before finishing its days at Llanelly shed. Photograph Stephen Gradidge.

An unlikely return for a pannier. Bristol Bath Road had been a diesel depot from the end of 1960 and afterwards a number of celebrated annual open days were held. It was almost the only chance you had to get in the place. The open days usually saw a few press-ganged steam locomotives and on 5 June 1965 one of the attendees, spruced up a bit, was 9680, a guest from Gloucester shed and still a working loco. 9680 survived until December 1965. Photograph Paul Chancellor Collection.

The highest numbered of the 96XXs, 9682, piloting 2-6-0 7305 on a down express through the late, lamented Birmingham Snow Hill station. This must be the latter part of the 1950s when 9682 was at Tyseley. A good 'working' pannier; dirt, grime, coal dust and plenty of water still draining off from the last fill up.

97XX

The condensing 97XX series were very different to look at, if that's not too obvious a statement to make. Tank capacity was increased by 30 gallons to 1,230 gallons but coal capacity was down to 2 tons 16 cwt, from 3 tons 6 cwt. Other obvious changes are the condensing piping and feed pump, the exposed smokebox and the tool box moved forward, let alone the curious circular vent in front of the dome. Their introduction saw the debut of the familiar and distinctive cabs with their rounded corners, cathedral-like windows and closing shutter for the cabside. This is 9700 at Old Oak (where they all spent much of their time, working down the Met lines to Smithfield as well as on empty stock) on 28 July 1963, three months before withdrawal and breaking up at Swindon. Photograph Stephen Gradidge.

9700 outside the 'factory' at Old Oak on 4 March 1956. When condensing, steam was forced back into the tanks and the vent in front of the dome was there for excess steam to escape; it would be very unwise to heat the tank water up to boiling! All condensing engines (the operation was often skipped as too tiresome) had large tank vents of one sort or another. All tanks of course have vents, but smaller than on a condensing engine, to prevent air being trapped at the top of the tank on the opposite side to the one at the column. Photograph Peter Groom.

9700 Old Oak 13/1/34; w/d 10/63
9701 Old Oak 9/33; Southall 4/1941; Old Oak 19/8/45; w/d 1/61
9702 Old Oak 9/33; Southall 12/1940; Old Oak 2/1941; w/d 5/62
9703 Old Oak 9/33; w/d 12/61
9704 Old Oak 10/33; w/d 11/63
9705 Old Oak 10/33; Southall 12/1940; Old Oak 2/1941; w/d 10/61
9706 Old Oak 12/33; w/d 11/64
9707 Old Oak 11/33; Southall 2/1941; Old Oak 19/8/45; Southall 30/11/63; Taunton 24/8/64*; w/d 9/64
9708 Old Oak 12/33; w/d 1/59
9709 Old Oak 12/33; Southall 3/1941; Old Oak 4/1941; w/d 5/62
9710 Old Oak 12/33; w/d 10/64
9711 Laira 30/6/34; Tondu 12/8/61; Radyr 19/5/62; Aberdare 9/2/63; Radyr 22/6/64; Gloucester 5/10/64; Bristol Barrow Road 27/3/65; w/d 7/65
9712 Newport Ebbw Jct 30/ 6/34; Aberdare by 12/34; w/d 9/62
9713 Severn Tunnel Jct 30/6/34; Newport Ebbw Jct 28/5/38; Aberbeeg 8/1942; Cardiff Canton 5/1943; Barry 8/9/62; Cardiff East Dock 9/2/63; Nine Elms 19/7/63; w/d 7/63
9714 Stafford Road 30/6/34; Shrewsbury 22/9/34; Stourbridge 2/5/38; Oxley 9/1940; Neyland 22/5/54; Fishguard Goodwick 25/2/61; w/d 11/61
9715 Shrewsbury 28/7/34; Oxley 23/7/38; Landore 11/8/56; Swansea East Dock 17/6/61; Duffryn Yard 15/7/61; Nine Elms 19/8/63; w/d 7/63
9716 Taunton 27/8/34; St. Blazey 20/10/34; Laira 2/5/38; St. Blazey 26/6/38; Laira 4/2/39; St. Blazey 10/9/60; Neath 8/9/62; w/d 6/65
9717 Newton Abbot 28/7/34; Exeter 15/10/38; Newton Abbot 12/11/38; Penzance 31/12/49; Hereford 4/12/54; w/d 12/62
9718 Exeter 28/7/34; St. Blazey 4/3/39; Laira 9/1941; Taunton 11/1942; w/d 5/62
9719 Stafford Road 28/7/34; Birkenhead 25/8/34; Shrewsbury 5/3/38; Chester 6/9/52; Stourbridge 4/10/52; w/d 7/62
9720 Yeovil 15/12/34; Westbury 12/1/35; Swindon 23/7/38; w/d 11/61
9721 St. Philips Marsh 15/12/34; Swindon 3/1942; w/d 6/62
9722 Oxford 15/12/34; Reading 1/6/35; Didcot 11/1944; Reading 23/2/46; Slough 4/11/50; w/d 7/62
9723 Aberbeeg 15/12/34; Newport Ebbw Jct 11/12/37; Llantrisant 20/8/38; Aberbeeg 17/5/47; Cardiff Canton 27/11/48; Pontypool Road 27/3/54; Cardiff Canton 24/4/54; Abercynon 14/7/62; w/d 7/62
9724 Tyseley 15/12/34; Leamington Spa 2/4/38; Tyseley 23/7/38; Oxley 12/10/39; Tyseley 11/11/39; Stafford Road 7/1943; Tyseley 8/1943; Stafford Road 19/4/47; Tyseley 17/5/47; Stourbridge 5/9/64; w/d 1/66
9725 Old Oak 15/12/34; w/d 12/62
9726 Old Oak 15/12/34; Southall 12/8/50; Old Oak 22/6/64; Didcot 20/7/64; Southall 10/1/65; w/d 6/65
9727 Stafford Road 15/12/34; Oxley 12/1/35; Tyseley 22/7/39; Worcester 11/1941; Gloucester 11/1942; Tyseley 9/9/50; Cardiff Canton 22/4/61; Barry 8/9/62; w/d 12/62
9728 Stourbridge 15/12/34; Oxley 21/8/37; Stourbridge 18/9/37; Stafford Road 7/1/39; Stourbridge 4/2/39; Banbury 11/11/39; Stafford Road 2/1941; Banbury 3/1941; Stafford Road 4/1941; Chester 5/1941; Stafford Road 4/1943; Chester 6/1943; Chester Midland 16/4/60; Abercynon 21/5/60; w/d 5/62
9729 St. Philips Marsh 15/12/34; Swindon 1/1941; St. Philips Marsh 5/1941; Bath Road 16/6/56; St. Philips Marsh 3/10/59; Westbury 3/11/63; w/d 10/64
9730 Stafford Road 12/1/35; Oxley 9/2/35; Wellington 3/1940; Oxley 5/1940; Pontypool Road 24/4/54; w/d 5/64
9731 Reading 12/1/35; Old Oak 9/2/35; Southall 23/7/38; Newport Ebbw Jct 10/1944; Aberdare 13/6/53; w/d 5/63
9732 Westbury 9/2/35; St. Philips Marsh 2/5/38; Yeovil Pen Mill 26/3/49; Yeovil Town 12/1/59; Swansea East Dock 30/11/63; w/d 4/64
9733 St. Philips Marsh 12/1/35; Oxley 15/10/38; Tyseley 1/1943; Leamington Spa 26/12/59; Tyseley 30/1/60; Stourbridge 15/7/61; w/d 9/65
9734 Neath 9/2/35; w/d 7/64
9735 Duffryn Yard 9/2/35; Landore 11/1940; Duffryn Yard 12/1940; w/d 3/61
9736 Duffryn Yard 9/2/35; w/d 6/61
9737 Duffryn Yard 9/2/35; w/d 12/60
9738 Landore 12/1/35; Tondu 30/1/60; w/d 1/62
9739 Stafford Road 9/2/35; Oxley 27/6/36; Wellington 18/9/37; Oxley 11/12/37; w/d 7/61
9740 Banbury 9/2/35; Wellington 6/3/37; Oxley 13/11/37; Stafford Road 8/1/38; Oxley 29/4/39; Leamington Spa 6/1942; Shrewsbury 22/3/52; Chester 25/2/56; Shrewsbury 24/3/56; Swindon 16/6/56; w/d 2/62
9741 Stafford Road 9/2/35; Oxley 9/3/35; Stourbridge 2/1941; Stafford Road 11/1944; Stourbridge 12/1944; Wellington 21/2/53; Worcester 23/3/57; Wellington 15/6/57; Shrewsbury 5/11/60; Wellington 3/12/60; w/d 8/62
9742 Leamington Spa 9/2/35; Oxley 7/1942; Wellington 24/3/51; Gloucester 23/3/57; Neath 13/4/64; w/d 9/64
9743 Llanelly 9/2/35; Neath 19/5/62; w/d 5/64
9744 Neath 9/2/35; Neyland 9/1/37; Llanelly 11/12/37; Swansea East Dock 22/7/39; Danygraig 8/9/56; Swansea East Dock 30/1/60; Llanelly 29/5/61; Swansea East Dock 19/5/62; w/d 1/63
9745 Severn Tunnel Jct 2/35; Newport Ebbw Jct 21/2/59; w/d 6/61
9746 Cardiff Canton 5/5/35; Newport Ebbw Jct 9/3/35; Llantrisant 11/1940; Cardiff Canton 12/1940; Aberbeeg 10/1942; Llantrisant 3/1944; Swansea East Dock 17/12/62; w/d 4/64
9747 Banbury 9/3/35; Stafford Road 24/7/37; Banbury 16/10/37; Oxley 3/1940; Cathays 2/2/54; Merthyr 11/9/54; Aberdare 12/1/63; w/d 1/63
9748 Stafford Road 9/3/35; Oxley 19/10/35; Wellington 16/11/35; Stafford Road 13/11/37; Wellington 11/12/37; Stafford Road 19/8/39; Chester 16/9/39; Tyseley 8/1941; Leamington Spa 5/1942; Tyseley 9/1942; Penzance 5/9/53; Neath 19/5/62; Neyland 6/4/63; Swansea East Dock 31/12/63; w/d 1/64
9749 Southall 9/3/35; Old Oak 26/6/38; Southall 12/11/38; Old Oak 10/12/38; Reading 7/1941; Swansea East Dock 8/10/60; w/d 11/60
9750 Taunton 29/6/35; Neath 27/5/39; w/d 5/62
9751 Taunton 29/6/35; Old Oak 29/4/39; w/d 6/61
9752 Stafford Road 29/6/35; Oxley 29/4/39; Swansea East Dock 21/4/62; w/d 12/63
9753 Tyseley 29/6/35; Stourbridge 7/3/36; Oxley 19/9/36; Tyseley 12/12/36; Leamington Spa 3/1941; Tyseley 9/1941; w/d 5/65
9754 Old Oak 29/6/35; Slough 15/10/38; Old Oak 10/12/38; Swindon 22/4/61; Westbury 9/2/63; Yeovil Town 27/3/65; w/d 6/65
9755 Southall 29/6/35; St. Blazey 23/4/49; Didcot 24/2/62; Old Oak 21/4/62; w/d 5/63
9756 Neath 27/7/35; Exmouth Jct 28/11/59; Weymouth 6/5/60; w/d 9/62
9757 Southall 27/7/35; Taunton 4/1939; Swansea East Dock 11/8/62; w/d 8/62
9758 Reading 27/7/35; Slough 9/1/37; Old Oak 29/5/37; Oxford 12/1943; Old Oak 2/1944; w/d 5/62
9759 Yeovil 27/7/35; Aberbeeg 3/2/40; Newport Ebbw Jct 10/1942; Cardiff Canton 11/1942; Abercynon 11/8/62; w/d 10/62
9760 Swansea East Dock 19/10/35; Fishguard Goodwick 12/1940; Duffryn Yard 29/9/63; w/d 12/63
9761 Llanelly 19/10/35; Landore; 12/11/38; Neath 9/9/50; Swansea East Dock 17/6/61; w/d 10/62
9762 Old Oak 19/10/35; Westbury 15/10/38; w/d 5/61
9763 Old Oak 19/10/35; Slough 7/1/39; Reading 10/1940; Old Oak 31/8/63; w/d 9/63
9764 St. Philips Marsh 19/10/35; Yeovil 24/3/51; Weymouth 17/5/52; Westbury 14/6/52; Yeovil Pen Mill 12/7/52; Yeovil 12/1/59; w/d 8/63
9765 St. Blazey 19/10/35; Exeter 5/1941; Laira 8/1941; Exeter 18/4/53; w/d 12/61
9766 Duffryn Yard 19/10/35; Neath 13/4/64; w/d 7/64
9767 Stafford Road 19/10/35; Salop 16/11/35; Shrewsbury 11/1/36; Oxley 29/4/39; Stourbridge 9/1940; w/d 6/61
9768 Tyseley 19/10/35; Stourbridge 24/6/39; Stafford Road 9/1940; Stourbridge 10/1940; Oxley 8/1941; w/d 12/64

9769 Stafford Road 19/10/35; Chester 16/11/35; Croes Newydd 17/9/38; Chester 15/10/38; Stafford Road 11/11/39; Oxley 9/12/39; Cardiff East Dock 27/2/54; Abercynon 13/7/57; Cathays 7/9/57; Cardiff East Dock 5/10/57; Bristol Bath Road 30/11/57; St. Philips Marsh 4/10/58; Westbury 8/10/60; w/d 3/63	
9770 Taunton 4/4/36; Laira 19/9/36; Nine Elms 11/3/59; Bath Green Park 27/7/63; w/d 12/63	
9771 St. Philips Marsh 4/4/36; Swindon 30/3/40; Yeovil 19/4/47; St. Philips Marsh 21/4/51; Bristol Bath Road 3/12/55; St. Philips Marsh 13/7/57; Bristol Bath Road 4/10/58; St. Philips Marsh 10/9/60; w/d 5/61	
9772 St. Philips Marsh 4/4/36; Bristol Bath Road 3/4/37; St Philips Marsh 13/11/37; Swindon 3/2/40; w/d 1/59	
9773 St. Philips Marsh 3/36; Swindon 4/3/39; Oxford 7/11/64; w/d 12/65	
9774 Banbury 4/4/36; Stourbridge 30/5/36; Stafford Road 12/11/38; Oxley 29/4/39; Wellington 6/1940; Stafford Road 3/1941; Chester 5/1941; Stafford Road 2/1942; Chester 6/1942; Wellington 11/7/53; Banbury 16/7/55; Wellington 8/10/55; Danygraig 8/9/56; Tyseley 5/9/64; w/d 11/66	
9775 Landore 4/4/36; Cardiff Canton 30/1/60; Barry 8/9/62; w/d 12/62	
9776 Landore 2/5/36; Gloucester 4/3/39; Barry 31/12/49; Cardiff East Dock 30/12/50; Abercynon 13/7/57; Cathays 7/9/57; Merthyr 29/11/58; Oxley 13/6/64; w/d 4/66	
9777 Swansea East Dock 2/5/36; Landore 11/1940; Duffryn Yard 2/1941; Landore 4/1941; Cardiff Canton 18/6/60; Landore 16/7/60; Neath 17/6/61; w/d 5/64	
9778 Severn Tunnel Jct 2/5/36; Cardiff Canton 1/11/47; Llantrisant 24/3/62; Radyr 26/10/64; w/d 11/64	
9779 Neyland 2/5/36; Neath 3/2/40; w/d 2/64	
9780 Tondu 25/7/36; Llantrisant 9/12/39; Barry 12/8/61; Tondu 9/2/63; Swansea East Dock 27/1/64; Neath 22/6/64; Radyr 6/2/65; w/d 7/65	
9781 Duffryn Yard 25/5/36; Fishguard Goodwick 22/8/36; Duffryn Yard 19/9/36; Didcot 12/1941; Slough 8/9/45; Didcot 25/3/61; w/d 5/61	
9782 Stafford Road 25/7/36; Banbury 10/12/38; Stourbridge 14/7/51; w/d 11/64	
9783 Duffryn Yard 257/36; Neath 22/8/36; w/d 5/62	
9784 St. Philips Marsh 25/7/36; Old Oak 22/7/39; w/d 5/63	
9785 Neath 30/5/36; Duffryn Yard 19/8/39; w/d 9/62	
9786 Neath 30/5/36; w/d 5/64	
9787 Llanelly 30/5/36; Carmarthen 10/8/57; Llanelly 31/8/63; Treherbert 29/9/63; w/d 9/64	
9788 Neath 30/5/36; Llanelly 27/6/36; Landore 20/3/48; Llanelly 7/8/48; Landore 27/11/48; Llanelly 26/3/49; Duffryn Yard 24/3/62; Neath 13/4/64; w/d 4/64	
9789 Old Oak 30/5/36; Slough 29/5/37; Old Oak 3/2/40; Slough 3/1940; Southall 24/3/56; Reading 27/1/62; Old Oak 31/8/63; Oxford 27/3/65; w/d 12/65	
9790 Swindon 27/6/36; Gloucester 7/11/64; Westbury 28/11/64; w/d 9/65	
9791 Old Oak 27/6/36; Reading 19/9/36; Southall 28/11/59; Didcot 24/2/62; w/d 1/64	
9792 Brecon 27/6/36; Neath 1/12/45; w/d 4/64	
9793 Stafford Road 27/6/36; Leamington Spa 11/11/39; Tyseley 3/2/40; Croes Newydd 16/6/51; w/d 8/63	
9794 Stourbridge 27/6/36; Stafford Road 12/1940; Chester 5/1943; Stafford Road 9/1943; Chester 10/1943; Chester Midland 16/4/60; Croes Newydd 21/5/60; Cardiff Canton 18/6/60; Barry 8/9/62; Cardiff East Dock 9/2/63; Barry 2/11/63; w/d 9/64	
9795 Westbury 19/9/36; Yeovil 5/2/38; Westbury 5/3/38; Swindon 8/1941; w/d 11/60	
9796 Newport Ebbw Jct 17/10/36; Aberbeeg 8/1/38; Cardiff Canton 2/1945; Aberbeeg 3/1945; Cardiff Canton 5/1945; Aberbeeg 15/7/50; Pontypool Road 29/11/52; w/d 2/65	
9797 Newport Ebbw Jct 17/10/36; Cardiff Canton 11/11/39; Aberbeeg 5/1941; Aberdare 10/1942; Aberbeeg 3/1944; Aberdare 8/1944; Aberbeeg 10/1944; Pontypool Road 23/3/46; w/d 9/62	
9798 Tyseley 17/10/36; Stafford Road 4/3/39; Tyseley 1/4/39; Stafford Road 12/7/52; Tyseley 29/11/52; Gloucester 12/1/63; Barry 31/12/63; w/d 10/64	
9799 Duffryn Yard 17/10/36; Neath 11/1940; Duffryn Yard 4/1941; w/d 10/63	
*9707: Believed to be a paper transfer [how many were there of those?] Locals never saw 9707 in or around Taunton at all.	

9701 in all its finery; the new black paint shows every rivet. The 'spare' lamp brackets and toolbox are set further forward on the running plate because of the extended tanks and the water filler on the tank top is set further back than on a conventional 57XX. That step set into the tank probably saw a leak or two over the years; note condensing mechanism rodding along lower part of smokebox. That prominent wheel under the bunker is the GW equivalent of the 'dump valve'; water in the tanks got hot in condensing work and if it got *too* hot the injectors would not work. So the contents were 'dumped' quickly at the nearest water column and the tanks refilled with cold water.

At a total of eleven, there were more than enough condensing panniers for the Metropolitan lines and they were to be found turn and turn about with the other panniers on the Old Oak-Paddington pilot jobs. 9701 is running in to Paddington on 4 March 1955 to collect an up train already berthed in the station. Tank filler lids left open; this was quite common and may have become a 'habit' with the condensing engines. Photograph Stephen Gradidge.

9702 on the approach road to the 'passenger side' at Old Oak, 17 July 1961; good look at the Weir pump and associated piping. The pump was there to replenish the boiler when the water in the unique tanks, part pannier and part side tank, had become too hot for the conventional injectors after receiving condensed exhaust steam but the 'dump valve' was still necessary – just in case. Note the extra step set neatly in the angle between the 'pannier' and the 'side' tank. Photograph Peter Groom.

9703 at Paddington on 4 March 1955; faded GWR on the side. Photograph Stephen Gradidge.

9704 in its last days at Old Oak, on 17 August 1962 a year before withdrawal. The loco is standing in front of the repair shop and there's a Western, D1004 WESTERN CRUSADER over on the right, on what served as the diesel roads in those early days. Photograph Peter Groom.

The end of 9704. This is the hulk in store at Southall on 8 March 1964, showing the shutter half closed. The loco had been withdrawn in November 1963 and was stored here (otherwise any move west of Old Oak, apart from works visits, seem to have been almost unheard of) for three months or so before disposal in June 1964. Photograph Stephen Gradidge.

9703 in a terrible state at Swindon with the steam dome stripped of its covering and tank vent at a drunken angle. It is no surprise that someone has chalked TAKE AWAY on the cab! There is unfortunately no date for this photograph but 9703 is not withdrawn: the 0-6-0 in front, 2274, was cut up at Swindon in October 1960 and the pannier wasn't withdrawn until December 1961. Old Oak must have been embarrassed to send it away like this! Photograph Paul Chancellor Collection.

9706, where else but at Old Oak, on 20 September 1963. It had just over a year to go and was the last of the condensers to be taken out of service, in November 1964. This was followed by what would have been its longest and final journey, to a South Wales scrapyard. Photograph Paul Chancellor Collection.

9707 bringing in the stock of a soon-to-be departure at Paddington in 1954.

9707 looking the worse for wear at Southall shed on 18 January 1964. It had moved there, regarded as just another pannier tank, the previous November though it is doubtful if much work was found for it; it was another 97XX scrapped in South Wales. Photograph Stephen Gradidge.

The condensing panniers did not acquire the high top feed it would seem. The piping and the exposed smokebox somehow gave them a more complicated and purposeful look. 9707, at Old Oak on 28 July 1963, has obviously just taken on water (note the usual open filler caps – that's the way you'd have to model one) ready for its next duty back to Paddington. It too was got rid of to Southall, like many of the surviving Old Oak stock, in November 1963. A bizarre 'paper' move followed, to Taunton in August 1964; locals who were around at the time swear it never made it to the west. Anyway it was withdrawn the following month. Photograph Stephen Gradidge.

Infernal vision at Old Oak, late in GW days. These are the 'fire pits' where ash and clinker was thrown out; the rickety structure behind was the shelter put up during the war to hide glowing fires from enemy aircraft at night. Both tanks have their numbers, 9709 and 9758, chalked on the front for parking in the roundhouse, the painted buffer beam numbers having long since faded. Photograph J.T. Clewley, www.transporttreasury.co.uk

The art of empty stock working at Paddington: 1. 9710 runs into the terminus to collect an up train on 1 September 1962. Tank filler lids open; Weir water pump obvious at the front. Unusually it is in the final BR livery, thanks to having received an overhaul at Caerphilly Works in February 1962. Photograph Stephen Gradidge.

The art of empty stock working at Paddington: 2. A little while later, 9710 begins the plod out to Old Oak with its train of stock. Photograph Stephen Gradidge.

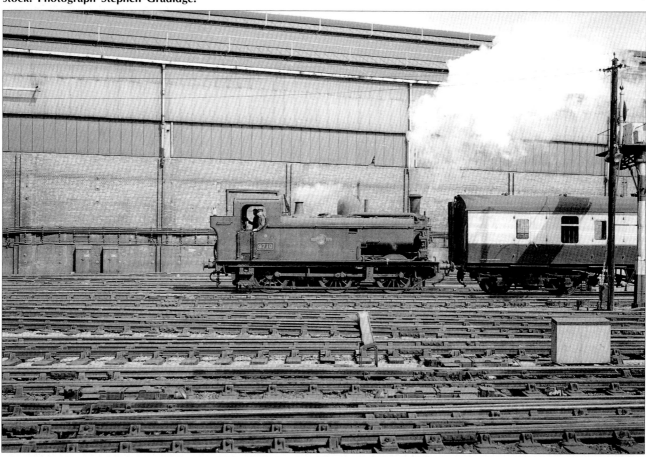

Three coaches, as ever. The next highest numbered after the condensers and we are a world away in June 1963 with 9711, then newly allocated to Radyr. It is out at work at Hengoed High Level on the Vale of Neath line. 9711 is on a service going forward to Pontypool Road, over the Crumlin viaduct. The bridge at the end of the platform is over the Rhymney Railway line from Rhymney to Cardiff; Hengoed Low Level lies below and to the right. In this case the primary route is the Vale of Neath line and the secondary route is the connection down to the Rhymney line north of Ystrad Mynach. Below the lower signal, masked by the station building, is a fixed distant, another GWR speciality. Photograph Paul Chancellor Collection.

On 2 September 1962 we have 9717 in all that jauntiness that a 57XX in decent nick could muster. It is at home at Hereford; it survived until the end of 1962. Photograph Stephen Gradidge.

9721 at Swindon, 12 August 1962. Photograph Stephen Gradidge.

9722 on 6 September 1952 at Langley, not far from its home shed Slough. Photograph Stephen Gradidge.

A 57XX very much in action. Stirring shot of 9724 bursting into Snow Hill station with a down freight, 30 July 1960. Photograph Michael Mensing.

9726, shutter partly closed, at home shed Southall on 21 July 1963. A padlocked engine. It moved to Old Oak in June 1964 and to Didcot the following month before returning to Southall in January 1965. It was withdrawn the following June. Photograph Stephen Gradidge.

9733 passes through Brierley Hill station with a short southbound freight on 26 August 1961. Driver, inexplicably, 'showing a leg'. Photograph Michael Mensing.

9735 at Duffryn Yard shed. A perfect workaday pannier; a bit cleaned, a bit grimy, a smattering of priming deposit. Photograph J. Davenport, Initial Photographics.

9736 of Duffryn Yard on a local goods working at Port Talbot on 14 March 1953; a time when simple railings were enough to separate running trains from the public. That washing looks vulnerable... Photograph Stephen Gradidge.

Gloriously grimy 9740 at Leamington shed. Photograph J. Davenport, Initial Photographics.

It was the sheer intimacy of (even) large sheds that made for so much of the attraction. At Wellington, from Victoria Street, engines were parked as if in next door's garden! This is 9741 on 2 September 1962 and though it is coaled up with fire iron and bucket on the bunker brackets and looking ready to go, its fate is already sealed and it awaits a move to a scrapyard. As mentioned already, electrification flashes, universally applied on say, the LMR (it made sense – that's where the electrification was going on) were, with good sense, not nearly so prevalent on the WR. Most of its locos, after all, were not even allowed on much of AC territory for reasons other than the wires. So, because 9741 might reasonably be expected to venture to Crewe, here is a 57XX with that rare thing, an electrification flash. A good view for once, of that roof grab iron and the ventilator. Photograph Stephen Gradidge.

Pleasing profile of 9744 at Danygraig on 2 August 1956, then its home shed. Emblem centrally placed for once; route availability/power disc very close to number plate. Photograph Stephen Gradidge.

9748, a Penzance engine far from home, at the west end of Canton roundhouse. In ex-works condition, it would have been to Caerphilly for attention and has paused here on the long way back home. Top feed boiler, disc higher, larger whistle shield, emblem well back. Even the lamp on the front is new. The higher numbered members of the class were completed by September 1936. Photograph Paul Chancellor Collection.

9753 on an up freight, east of West Bromwich station, 20 September 1958. Photograph Michael Mensing.

9759 outside the roundhouse at Canton; emblem near centrally placed, aligned with the dome, weld patches on tank. Photograph J. Davenport, Initial Photographics.

One of the SR exiles; 9770 at Nine Elms on 25 May 1963 where it spent nearly four and a half years. During this time it had one visit to Ashford Works and two to Eastleigh, the last in June 1962 where the WR type ATC was removed and the BR AWS fitted instead – the battery box is under the bunker. In July 1963 it moved back to the WR. Photograph Stephen Gradidge.

Up short freight standing at the south end of Birmingham Snow Hill, 5 May 1966; 9774 with those curious stencilled 'diesel' style numbers, just like D1585 on the right, in fact. The photographer notes mournfully that 'This was the last GW engine I ever saw in everyday service – months after the previous sighting.' Photograph Michael Mensing.

Forlorn and abandoned at Swindon in March 1963, three months after withdrawal, 9775 sits among the clinker of its last fire. Scrapping came in June 1963. Photograph Stephen Gradidge.

9784 in good condition at Old Oak Common on 1 March 1959. Top feed boiler, toolbox locked, second BR emblem. Photograph Peter Groom.

9789 at Old Oak in September 1963 looking thoroughly the worse for wear – worse in fact than some of the withdrawn examples we've seen. Yet there were still a couple of years in the old girl; a final move to Oxford came in April 1965. Photograph Stephen Gradidge.